Sports Illustrated KIDS

ATHLETES FOR
GENDER EQUITY

BILLIE JEAN KING, THE U.S. WOMEN'S SOCCER TEAM, AND MORE

by Jaclyn Jaycox

CAPSTONE PRESS
a capstone imprint

Published by Capstone Captivate, an imprint of Capstone.
1710 Roe Crest Drive, North Mankato, Minnesota 56003
capstonepub.com

Library of Congress Cataloging-in-Publication Data is available on the Library
of Congress website.
ISBN: 9781663965950 (hardcover)
ISBN: 9781666321272 (paperback)
ISBN: 9781666321289 (ebook pdf)

Summary: From tennis legend Billie Jean King to the U.S. Women's Soccer Team,
athletes have fought for equity and fairness for women in professional sports.
Discover the pro athletes who have used their platforms to speak out and affect
change for all women.

Image Credits
Alamy: AF archive, 11, ZUMA Press, 23; Getty Images: Boston Globe/Contributor,
7, PA Images/Contributor, 4, Simon Hofmann/Stringer, 8; Newscom: Ahmad
Massoud Xinhua News Agency, 27 (bottom), EFE/Alejandro Garcia, 27 (top),
Icon Sportswire/Jevone Moore, 25, Icon Sportswire/Ken Murray, 24, Image of
Sport Photos, 28, Reuters/Christian Hartmann, 29, ZUMA Press/Karen Wilson,
19; Shutterstock: HelloSSTK, Cover; Sports Illustrated: Bob Martin/Contributor,
17, 21, Erick W. Rasco/Contributor, 5, Neil Leifer/Contributor, 15, Robert Beck/
Contributor, 12, 13

Editorial Credits
Editor: Erika L. Shores; Designer: Heidi Thompson; Media Researcher: Jo Miller;
Production Specialist: Tori Abraham

Printed and bound in the USA. PO4608

TABLE OF CONTENTS

Words in BOLD appear in the glossary.

INTRODUCTION

Once upon a time, girls were not allowed to play professional sports. Women were considered weaker than men. Playing sports was just a hobby for women. Their job was to have children and take care of the home. But many female athletes refused to let their talents go to waste. They began fighting for equity, or fair and equal treatment, in sports.

Tennis star Billie Jean King fought for equal prize money to that of male tennis stars in the 1970s.

Female athletes have experienced lower pay than men. They also get less **publicity** and fewer opportunities. There's more work to be done for an equal future. But many brave women have stood up for what they believe in. They've used their voices and their talents to make big changes in the world of sports.

Tennis superstar Serena Williams continues to speak out for equity in sports.

FIGHTING TO PLAY

Some athletes had to become **activists** just to compete. These female athletes fought to get their sport included on the same stage as male athletes.

KATHRINE SWITZER

Kathrine Switzer was a college student who loved to run. At 20 years old, Switzer decided to register for the 1967 Boston Marathon. Back then, women were not allowed to take part. She entered by using her initials. Her **gender** was not obvious because she did not use Kathrine.

On the day of the race, an official ran after Switzer. He tried to rip off her bib number. He yelled at her to get out of the race. Her boyfriend pushed him away. Switzer kept running and finished the race. Her story was shared in the newspapers. She became an activist for female runners. In 1972, women were officially allowed to run in the Boston Marathon. Switzer went on to successfully fight to include a women's marathon in the Olympics.

An official (behind Switzer) tried to remove Kathrine Switzer's bib number and stop her from running in the Boston Marathon.

LINDSEY VAN

Lindsey Van dreamed of competing in ski jumping in the Olympics. But there was not a ski jump event for women. Van was part of a lawsuit arguing the sport should be included in the 2010 Olympic Games. She didn't win the lawsuit, but she kept fighting. Finally, it was added for the 2014 Games. Because of Van, women ski jumpers now have the chance at an Olympic medal.

Lindsey Van com
in the ski jump.

FLOR ISAVA-FONSECA

Flor Isava-Fonseca was a national champion in tennis and **equestrian** in her country of Venezuela. She was a member of the Venezuelan equestrian team at the 1956 Olympics.

Isava-Fonseca wanted to see more events for women in the Olympics. In 1981, she became one of the first women members of the International Olympic Committee (IOC). Nine years later, she was the first woman to be elected to the IOC Executive Board. She faced **discrimination** along the way. But she never quit working to increase women's representation in sports.

FACT

Flor Isava-Fonseca not only competed in tennis and horseback riding, but also swimming, hockey, and golf.

KATHRYN BERTINE

Kathryn Bertine is a professional cyclist. The Tour de France is a world-famous cycling race. But it was only open to men. Bertine **petitioned** for five years to get an equal event for women. In 2014, her work paid off. She competed in the first Tour de France race for women.

Bertine made a documentary called *Half the Road*. It highlights the problems of unequal pay and representation in cycling.

In 2015, Bertine started the Homestretch Foundation. It provides free housing to female athletes who are struggling financially.

FACT

Kathryn Bertine is also an author of five books. In 2021, she published *Stand: A Memoir on Activism. A Manual for Progress.*

Kathryn Bertine raced on World Tour teams from 2012 to 2017.

RONDA ROUSEY

Ronda Rousey learned the sport of judo when she was young. She earned a bronze medal at the 2008 Olympics. She retired from judo and started competing in mixed martial arts (MMA). But it was difficult to be a woman in this sport.

In 2011, the Ultimate Fighting Championship (UFC) president said women would never fight in the UFC. Rousey would soon change everything. In 2012, she became the first woman to sign with the UFC. Other women soon followed. Rousey went undefeated for more than two years. In 2018, she became the first woman **inducted** into the UFC Hall of Fame.

Ronda Rousey holds her Olympic medal for judo in 2008.

Ronda Rousey in action during the first Women's UFC fight in 2013

EQUAL PRIZE MONEY

Athletes at the top of their game earn huge payouts for winning. Winning a championship title can bring in millions of dollars in prizes. But when it comes to female athletes, the payout is often much different from male athletes in the same sport.

BILLIE JEAN KING

Billie Jean King is a retired professional tennis player. She has dozens of championship titles under her belt. But she won far less in prize money than male players. In 1973, she successfully fought for equal pay at the U.S. Open. It was the first major tournament to pay men and women equally.

King became famous for winning the "Battle of the Sexes" tennis match in 1973. Her opponent was Bobby Riggs. He didn't believe women could play tennis as well as men. She proved him, and the world, wrong. King continues her fight for women's rights today.

The "Battle of the Sexes" tennis match attracted more than 90 million viewers worldwide. It is the most watched tennis match in history.

Billie Jean King (bottom) beat Bobby Riggs in the "Battle of the Sexes" match in Houston, Texas.

VENUS WILLIAMS

Venus Williams followed in Billie Jean King's footsteps. The U.S. Open, Australian Open, and French Open all paid men and women equal prize money. Wimbledon was the only major tournament still paying women less. Williams wrote a newspaper article about it in 2006. By 2007, her work paid off. She became the first female Wimbledon champion to be paid the same as a man.

CARMELITA JETER

Carmelita Jeter is a retired U.S. sprinter. She won three medals at the 2012 Olympic Games. She also won the title of Fastest Woman Alive. She teamed up with Nike to help train young female track and field athletes. She is also teaching them to fight for what they believe in. She didn't receive as much pay as men. But she hopes her activism helps other female athletes do so.

FACT

The *Forbes*' list of the highest paid athletes in 2020 is made up mostly of men. Tennis players Naomi Osaka and Serena Williams are the only two women in the top 50 spots.

Venus Williams shows off her Wimbledon trophy in 2007.

BIANCA VALENTI

Bianca Valenti is a professional big wave surfer. In 2014, she entered a big wave competition. There was a prize of $50,000 for the men. But the eight women that participated had to split $5,000.

In 2016, Valenti teamed up with other female surfers. They formed the Committee for Equity in Women's Surfing (CEWS). They were successful in getting more women's surfing events added. In 2018, Valenti was the first Women's Big Wave Champion at the Puerto Escondido Cup. That same year, the CEWS got the World Surf League to start paying equal prize money.

Bianca Valenti competes in
a women's longboard event
in France in 2006.

SERENA WILLIAMS

Serena Williams is one of the best tennis players of all time. Twice she has held all four major titles at the same time. No other player—man or woman—has ever done that. But she makes less money than male players. Williams has experienced inequality as a woman and as a Black person. She has been a huge advocate for equal rights.

In 2020, Williams joined with Secret Deodorant on a study about gender bias in sports. Gender bias is unequal treatment of men and women. The study wants to discover where the inequalities start. Then people can find ways to fix them. Williams hopes this will lead to big changes for female athletes.

Even though Serena Williams has won more championships, she still makes less money than many successful male pro athletes.

BRANDS BACKING WOMEN

Many companies have stepped up to support female athletes and their quest for equality. Secret Deodorant has spent more than $1 million to help this cause. They bought and donated more than 9,000 tickets to the National Women's Soccer League games. Nike has supported female coaches and funded a number of projects that help young girls play sports. Roxy started a campaign to encourage all girls to follow their dreams in both sports and life.

INVESTING IN WOMEN'S SPORTS

Female athletes experience inequality that goes beyond prize money or **salaries**. For most female athletes and their teams, they receive less benefits and publicity. But there are plenty of female athletes willing to work for change.

U.S. WOMEN'S SOCCER

The U.S. Women's Soccer Team won the World Cup in 2015. The final game had more than 25 million viewers. It was the most watched soccer game in history. The men's team had never won a World Cup. Yet they were paid much more. The women were tired of unequal pay and working conditions. In 2019, they sued the U.S. Soccer Federation for gender discrimination.

Members of the U.S. Women's Soccer Team
before a World Cup match in October 2014

The following year, the U.S. Soccer Federation
agreed to make changes. The women will play
on better fields. They will also have better travel
accommodations. They didn't win equal pay, but
they are continuing that fight. They are standing
up for themselves and for future female soccer
players.

U.S. WOMEN'S HOCKEY

In 2017, the U.S. Women's Hockey Team planned to **boycott** the World Championships. For more than a year they had been asking for equal treatment as the men's teams. This led to historic changes for women's hockey. They got a four-year agreement with increased pay. They will also get bonuses for winning world championships or Olympic titles. USA Hockey also made improvements in how they schedule and promote women's games.

The U.S. Women's Hockey Team at the 2018 Winter Olympics

NNEKA OGWUMIKE

Nneka Ogwumike plays basketball for the Los Angeles Sparks. She is also president of the Women's National Basketball Association (WNBA) Players Association. She fights for equality for her fellow female athletes. They wanted more money and better benefits for players in their league. In 2020, an agreement was reached. Players got pay increases. They will now be paid when taking time off to have a baby. The WNBA will also invest money into childcare and housing for players with children.

Nneka Ogwumike plays for the Los Angeles Sparks.

OVERCOMING ALL ODDS

Some athletes faced big challenges in their efforts for equality. But they fought hard for what they believed in. These athletes have helped lead the way for all female athletes.

KHALIDA POPAL

Khalida Popal grew up in Afghanistan. She helped start a national women's soccer team there. But it wasn't easy. In her country, soccer is a man's game. People would yell and throw garbage at her. But she didn't let that stop her.

Popal was named the first captain of the female team in 2007. She became an advocate for women's rights. Because of this, she received death threats. For her safety, she left the country in 2011. Even though she was gone, she was not silenced. Popal started an organization called Girl Power. It aims to help girls across Europe and the Middle East participate in sports.

In 2019, Khalida Popal spoke about her work to start a women's soccer team in Afghanistan.

The Afghan women's national soccer team in 2011

ALYSIA MONTANO

Alysia Montano ran in the U.S. Track and Field Championships in 2014. She was eight months pregnant. Three years later, she ran the same race at five months pregnant. Many women runners lose **sponsorships** when they become pregnant. Montano wanted to change that. She started a nonprofit to help in cases like hers. She believes women athletes should be able to be mothers and still have a career.

Alysia Montano running in the 800-meter race in 2014.

ALANA NICHOLS

Alana Nichols was paralyzed in a snowboarding accident at 17 years old. But she didn't let this stop her from doing what she loved. She became a three-sport Paralympic athlete. In January 2020, she became president of the Women's Sports Foundation. They work to advance gender equity in sports. She believes all girls, no matter what their abilities are, should be able to play sports.

Nichols won a silver
in alpine downhill skiing.

GLOSSARY

accommodation (uh-kaa-muh-DAY-suhn)—lodging, food, and other services

activist (AK-tiv-ist)—a person who works for social or political change

boycott (BOY-kaht)—to refuse to take part in something as a way of making a protest

discrimination (dis-kri-muh-NAY-shuhn)—treating people unfairly because of their race, country of birth, or gender

equestrian (ih-KWES-tree-uhn)—having to do with horseback riding

gender (JEHN-dur)—male or female

induct (in-DUHKT)—to take in as an official member of an organization or group

inequality (in-ee-KWA-luh-tee)—being unequal

petition (puh-TISH-uhn)—to make a formal request

publicity (puh-BLI-suh-tee)—public attention or interest

salary (SAL-uh-ree)—money paid on a regular schedule to people doing a job

sponsorship (SPON-sur-ship)—financial support of a person, event, or project, usually in return for public acknowledgment

READ MORE

Kortemeier, Todd. *Greatest Female Athletes of All Time.* Minneapolis: Abdo Publishing, 2018.

McKinney, Donna B. *Women in Soccer.* Lake Elmo, MN: Focus Readers, 2020.

Weintraub, Aileen. *We Got Game!: 35 Female Athletes Who Changed the World.* Philadelphia: Running Press Kids, 2020.

INTERNET SITES

KidsHealth: 5 Reasons for Girls to Play Sports
kidshealth.org/en/teens/girls-sports.html

Sports Illustrated Kids: The Debate Over Equal Pay in Tennis, Explained
www.sikids.com/tennis/equal-pay-raymond-moore-billie-jean-king-venus-williams-novak-djokovic-andy-murray

TIME for Kids: Play for Equality
timeforkids.com/g34/play-for-equality/

INDEX

ABOUT THE AUTHOR

Jaclyn Jaycox is a children's book author and editor. When she's not writing, she loves reading and spending time with her family. She lives in southern Minnesota with her husband, two kids, and a spunky goldendoodle.